Community Helpers

Child Care Workers

By Karen Bush Gibson

Consultant:
Megan Shaw
Editor, *Early Childhood News*

Bridgestone Books
an imprint of Capstone Press
Mankato, Minnesota

Bridgestone Books are published by Capstone Press
151 Good Counsel Drive, P.O. Box 669, Mankato, Minnesota 56002
http://www.capstone-press.com

Library of Congress Cataloging-in-Publication Data
Gibson, Karen Bush.
    Child Care Workers/by Karen Bush Gibson.
    p. cm.—(Community helpers)
    Includes bibliographical references and index.
    Summary: Introduces the responsibilities, equipment, necessary schooling, and
different kinds of people who take care of children.
    ISBN 0-7368-0622-9
    1. Child care workers—Juvenile literature. [1. Child care workers. 2. Occupations.]
I. Title. II. Community helpers (Mankato, Minn.)
HQ778.5 .G5 2001
362.71'2—dc21   00-023629

Editorial Credits
Sarah L. Schuette, editor; Timothy Halldin, cover designer; Katy Kudela,
    photo researcher

Photo Credits
David F. Clobes, 10
Index Stock Imagery, 16
James L. Shaffer, 8
Leslie O'Shaughnessy, 4, 6
Lois Roberts, 14
Photo Agora/Gerard Fritz, cover; Jeff Greenberg, 20
Unicorn Stock Photos/N.P. Alexander, 18
Visuals Unlimited/Inga Spence, 12

1 2 3 4 5 6 06 05 04 03 02 01

Table of Contents

Child Care Workers

Child care workers take care of children when their parents are away. These workers are responsible for babies and young children. Child care workers make sure children are safe.

responsible
able to do important duties

What Child Care Workers Do

Child care workers help children learn and develop. Child care workers plan fun things for children to do. They make meals and snacks. Child care workers help children solve problems.

develop
to grow and change

When Child Care Workers Work

Child care workers work whenever parents need help with their children. Child care workers work during the day or at night. They sometimes work on weekends.

Where Child Care Workers Work

Child care workers work in homes, child care centers, and schools. They sometimes set up child care businesses in their own homes.

Nannies

A nanny is a child care worker who works with one family. Nannies sometimes live in the family's home. They play with children and prepare meals for them.

Tools Child Care Workers Use

Child care workers provide books for learning. They provide toys for play. Child care workers know how to use safety equipment such as fire extinguishers and first aid kits.

fire extinguisher
a holder with water and chemicals inside it used to put out fires

Child Care Workers and School

Child care workers learn about children by spending time with them. They also take classes to learn first aid. Some child care workers have a college degree in early childhood education.

degree
a title; students earn a degree after finishing certain classes at a college or university.

People Who Help Child Care Workers

Government workers check child care centers and homes to make sure they are safe. Parents help child care workers by telling them what their children need.

government

the people who rule or govern a country or a state

How Child Care Workers Help Others

Child care workers and parents work together to keep children safe. Child care workers help children have fun. They teach children about each other and the world around them.

Hands On: Snack Time

Child care workers often make snacks for children. You can make a snack and share it with your friends.

What You Need

Dry measuring cup
1 cup raisins
1 cup peanuts or sunflower seeds
1 cup pretzel sticks
1 cup small chocolate candies or candy corn
Large bowl
Wooden spoon
Small plastic bags

What You Do

1. Measure all of the ingredients and put them in a large bowl.
2. Mix all of the ingredients together with the wooden spoon.
3. Divide the mixture into small plastic bags.
4. Share the snack with your friends.

Words to Know

degree (di-GREE)—a title; students earn a degree after finishing certain classes at a college or university.

develop (di-VEL-uhp)—to grow and change; children develop as they get older.

fire extinguisher (FIRE ik-STING-gwi-sher)—a holder with water and chemicals inside it; people use fire extinguishers to put out fires.

government (GUHV-urn-muhnt)—the people who rule or govern a country or state; government workers check child care centers.

responsible (ri-SPON-suh-buhl)—able to do important duties; child care workers are responsible for children.

Read More

Quinlan, Kathryn A. *Child Care Worker.* Careers without College. Mankato, Minn.: Capstone Books, 1999.

Raatma, Lucia. *Responsibility.* Character Education. Mankato, Minn.: Bridgestone Books, 1999.

Weintraub, Aileen. *Careers in Child Care.* World of Work. New York: Rosen, 2000.

Internet Sites

Kids Health
http://kidshealth.org/kid/index.html
National Child Care Information Center
http://nccic.org

Index

Reader Commun

j362.71   Gibson, Karen Bush.
GIB   Child care workers.

$18.60   02/24/2003

DATE			

BAKER & TAYLOR